Let's Be Friends

A Workbook to Help Kids Learn Social Skills & Make Great Friends

LAWRENCE E. SHAPIRO, PH.D.
JULIA HOLMES

Instant Help Books
A Division of New Harbinger Publications, Inc.

Distributed in Canada by Raincoast Books

Instant Help Books
A Division of New Harbinger Publications, Inc.
5674 Shattuck Avenue
Oakland, CA 94609
www.newharbinger.com

Cover design by Amy Shoup

Illustrations by Julie Olson

Cover photo is a model used for illustrative purposes only.

Library of Congress Cataloging-in-Publication Data on file with publisher

Printed in the United States of America

24 23 22

20 19 18 17 16

Contents

A Note to Parents

Many children today have problems making and keeping friends. They are left out of games at recess. They don't get invited to other children's houses for playdates. They may be teased by other children or just be avoided.

It can be upsetting for parents to realize that their children are having trouble making friends while other children seem to have active social lives. The solution is simple: teach your children the specific emotional and social skills they need to connect with their peers, using the fun and informative activities found in this book. Once learned, these skills will last a lifetime.

Children do not have to acquire every skill before they will be able to solve the problem of social isolation. In fact, learning even one new skill by doing just one of the forty activities in this book may do the trick. Look through the book before you start using it with your child and see if there are specific things your child will benefit from knowing.

The activities are based on the theory of emotional intelligence, which assumes that emotional, behavioral, and social skills can be learned in much the same way as sports, music, or academic skills. Each activity begins by highlighting important information children need to know about making friends. The next section provides an activity that will teach more about this skill, while the final section poses questions to help children think about what they have learned. Children can answer these questions out loud, but it will be most helpful if they write down their answers, with your help, if necessary. When you keep written responses in the book, you can go back to them at a later date and see if your child has learned something new or still has the same thoughts and beliefs.

While many of the activities can be done by children alone, they will be more effective when an adult provides guidance. You probably know from your own experience that changing one's behavior is not easy, and your support will definitely help.

This book is a starting point for you to help your child make friends. The real learning will take place out of your sight as your child applies the lessons in new situations with peers. But that doesn't mean your involvement stops when you close this book. You can continue to be a social coach, encouraging your child to keep trying new ideas, thinking about how they are working, and seeking out new friends.

You may find that it is difficult for your child to talk about certain issues. Never force a child who doesn't want to talk. The best way to get children to open up is to be a good role model. Talk about your thoughts, feelings, and experiences as they relate to each activity, stressing the positive ways that you cope with problems. Even if your child doesn't say a thing in response, your words will have an impact.

If your child continues to have difficulty with peers after trying some of the activities in this book, consider getting professional guidance. Some children have difficulty making friends because their brains are simply not wired the same way as other children's. They may not be able to read body language or they may have emotional difficulties that affect their ability to make friends. They may have problems managing their anger. They may have an anxiety disorder that makes it hard for them to be in new situations. Or they may have problems with empathy and find it difficult to see things from another person's point of view. These issues can all be helped with the aid of a professional counselor, and if you are concerned about your child's social development, you should certainly consult with the school psychologist in your area. There are many ways to assess whether a child has a problem that needs treatment or whether extra support at home will do the trick.

If your child does need professional help, you will find this workbook to be of added benefit. Show it to your child's counselor, who may have some additional ideas on the best way to use it.

There is no wrong way to use this workbook as long as you remain patient and respectful of your child's feelings. We wish you success in the most important job in the world—being a good parent.

Sincerely,

The Authors

Introduction for Kids

Someone probably gave you this book because you are having trouble making friends. If this is the case, don't feel bad. Lots of kids find it hard to make friends at one time or another. This book will give you some great ideas to help you make friends and have lots of fun doing it.

Do you remember when you first learned to ride a bike or when you first learned to swim? It was hard at first, but with practice you got better. It's the same way when it comes to learning how to make friends.

There are forty activities in this book that will teach you many things about making friends. You will learn how to have a friendly manner so that other kids will like being with you. You will learn how read body language so that you can recognize how other kids are feeling. And you will learn the secrets which few kids know, of handling teasing or criticism.

We hope that you find this book interesting and helpful and that you make lots and lots of new friends.

Good luck and have fun!

The Authors

Section I: Making Friends

Some kids are outgoing and talkative, but other kids are shy and quiet when anyone is around. Some kids are good at sports and make friends on their teams. Other kids are not good at sports, and they don't like to be on teams.

Everyone is different, but everyone can make friends! The trick is to find friends who like you for who you are and who enjoy doing the same kind of things as you.

The activities in this section will help you to think about who you are and to let others know what is special about you. They will also help you think about what qualities make kids most likely to be good friends.

Activity 1 About You

For You to Know

Kids who know a lot about themselves have an easier time finding the right friends.

You are truly an individual. You are like nobody else! You have a combination of talents, friendships, skills, likes, dislikes, plans, and experiences that are different from anyone else's. People are always changing, so it would be impossible to sum up *everything* about any one person. But the more you know about yourself, the better you can be at making friends. Thinking about what interests you, what you are good at, and what's important to you can help. To get started, take a look at yourself!

For You to Do

Draw a picture of yourself in the space below. You might want to draw yourself doing your favorite activity, with some of your favorite people or animals, or surrounded by some things you love. It's up to you.

Name ______________________________ Age ____________

Activity 1 About You

What does your picture say about you?

____

____

____

____

____

What do you think is the most important thing about this picture?

____

____

____

____

____

... *And More to Do!*

These are the people in my family:______________________________

____

____

My favorite book is ______________________________________

My favorite movie is _____________________________________

My favorite kind of music is _______________________________

My favorite animal is _____________________________________

My favorite food is ______________________________________

My favorite sport is ______________________________________

I am really good at ______________________________________

I'd like to be better at ____________________________________

I care a lot about _______________________________________

When I am older, I would like to ______________________________

Activity 2 Finding Shared Interests

For You to Know

Most kids find it easier to become friends when they have things in common, like loving to read or to ride bikes. Doing things you both like is a great way of getting to know a new friend. New friends can even help you discover new interests to share!

William walked through the double doors of his new school. Everything about the building seemed giant. It was at least four times the size of his old school. The classroom doors towered over him, and even the kids looked bigger. He felt as if he were walking into a whole new world, where nothing was familiar. He wanted to make friends but was worried that he would not have anything in common with the new kids.

That day at lunch, William looked around for kids who seemed friendly. When a boy from his class waved at him, William headed over and asked, "Can I sit with you?" The kids at the table were talking about a movie they had all seen. Amanda said it was the best movie ever. William agreed, and then asked "Did anyone read the book?" Trevor said he had. He and William agreed that they both liked the book a lot, but thought the movie was better. Ethan said, "We're all going to the movies on Saturday. Do you want to come with us?"

William smiled. He was on his way to making friends.

For You to Do

Write a short letter to an imaginary pen pal describing one thing you enjoyed about last summer. It can be something you did or saw, or something that happened to you. Be sure to ask questions about your pen pal's summer.

... And More to Do!

Think of someone who is important to you and whom you feel close to. What do you most admire about this person?

____

____

What four words would you use to describe this person?

1. ____________________ 3. ____________________

2. ____________________ 4. ____________________

Write down at least two things you have in common with this person.

____

____

What are some ways you are different from one another?

____

____

What would you like to learn from this person?

____

____

What could you teach this person?

____

____

Where to Meet New Friends

For You to Know

You can meet new friends in many different ways. One easy way is through interests you share. It's also a good idea to be open-minded, because you may find that people you don't expect to like can become your good friends.

Ryan and Cody were in different classes, and they didn't know one another well. In fact, they had never even had a conversation, and Ryan thought Cody looked kind of geeky—not the kind of kid he would want to be friendly with.

Ryan was responsible for walking his dog every day after school. He often saw Cody out at the same time, walking his dog. One afternoon, the two dogs started to play, and the two boys talked about their dogs. The next week at school, there was an announcement about a new gymnastics club. Ryan and Cody both showed up at the first meeting. After the meeting, they talked about their favorite Olympic gymnasts, and Ryan found himself realizing that Cody was really cool and not geeky at all.

For You to Do

Look through old magazines, newspapers, and catalogs for pictures of activities and places where you are likely to find kids who share your interests. Use the pictures to make a collage in this space.

... *And More to Do!*

Think of two friends who are very important to you today. Where did you meet them?

___

___

Where have you met most of your friends?

___

___

Write about the most unexpected way you met someone who became a good friend. Tell what you were doing, what your first reaction to this person was, and how you started your friendship.

___

___

___

___

___

Activity 4 Friendly Kids Make Friends

For You to Know

We all like to be around friendly people, and it's easier to get to know kids who act friendly. Being greeted by someone in a friendly way immediately makes you feel good, both about yourself and the other person.

Part of being friendly is showing other kids that you are happy to be with them and that you are interested in them. Being friendly also means giving other kids the chance to learn more about you—your interests, your sense of humor, what you like to do, and how you think. And learning more about each other makes it easier to become friends.

Think about how you would feel if you said hello to a new boy in your class and he just stood there, staring down at his shoes, arms folded across his chest. Then think about how you would react if he smiled and said hello back to you.

Saying hello, asking how someone is, offering to help, making eye contact, and having a relaxed attitude all let kids know that you are friendly. Once they see that you are friendly, it will be easier for them to relax and be friendly, too.

For You to Do

Jan has just started going to a new after-school program. She recognizes some of the kids, but doesn't know any of them well. None of the kids from her class are in the program. Though she has friends in her own class, she wants to have good friends to spend time with after school, too.

Below are three scenes from the after-school program. Can you help Jan think of ways to be friendly to new kids?

Put a check mark on the picture of the kids that Jan should talk to first. Tell why you chose that group.

___

___

What is one thing Jan might say when she approaches these kids?

___

___

What can Jan do to let the other kids know that she wants to be friends with them?

___

___

___

... And More to Do!

What makes you think of other kids as friendly?

What kinds of things do friendly kids say or do?

Tell about a time when you wanted to be friends with someone. How did you let that person know?

Making a Good First Impression

Activity 5

For You to Know

Making a good first impression can help a lot when you are getting to know other kids. Try your best, but don't worry if you feel like you didn't make a good first impression. You can change what you do the next time!

Kyle loved music. He like to read it, to play it, and to write new songs. He had been practicing the keyboard for months, using his older brother's keyboard. He was eager to meet other kids who were as excited about music as he was. Even though he felt shy, he decided to sign up for the school band. Once he got there, though, his shyness got the better of him. He wasn't sure what to say to the other kids, especially since they all seemed to know one another. He felt lonely and sad.

When he got home, his brother asked how things had gone. Kyle said, "It was awful. Nobody talked to me. I stood alone the whole time and I felt miserable."

"And you probably looked miserable," added his brother. "Would you go up to someone who looked like he *wanted* to be left alone? I bet if you had said hello to one person, or asked someone else about their instrument, things would have been a lot more fun." When his brother headed out to play basketball, Kyle decided to practice looking friendlier and more relaxed.

At the next band meeting, he smiled at the boy next to him and asked how long he had been in the band. The two boys got into a great conversation and found out that they both had the same favorite group.

For You to Do

Practice looking in the mirror and saying hello to yourself in different ways. You may feel a bit goofy at first, but give it a try. Write down a brief description of each way you try.

____

____

____

____

Try frowning at yourself in the mirror. How does that make you feel?

____

____

Which way of saying hello do you think would be the best choice? Tell why.

____

____

____

… And More to Do!

What do you look for when you first meet other kids?

____

____

____

____

How would your friends or family members describe you?

____

____

____

____

List four words that other people might use to describe your personality.

1. ____________________ 3. ____________________

2. ____________________ 4. ____________________

Activity 6 Being Popular for Life

For You to Know

Lots of people are popular for a short period of time—a few weeks or a summer. That kind of popularity is sometimes based on being mean to others or excluding them, and the friendships it leads to don't usually last. Real popularity involves good friendships that last for years, and it comes from making other people feel good about themselves.

Nora always got what she wanted, and no one ever got in her way. She seemed to have a lot of friends, but these kids didn't really feel good being around her. They were just relieved when she was being nice to them and mean to others. Everyone was nervous around Nora, always trying to stay on her good side and hoping that they wouldn't be the target of her nasty remarks. If kids were on Nora's good side, and she was being especially sweet to them, they felt special. But by the end of the week, Nora would change again.

When Jared first came to school as a new kid, he smiled and said hello to Nora, but she just stared at him and turned away. By the end of the semester, Jared had started a band with other kids from school and they won the school talent contest. He had run for class president, and won. He was friendly to *everyone*.

Nora tried gossiping about him with the other kids, but this time she didn't get her way. Jared had tried hard to make friends, and when he made them, they seemed to be friends for life.

For You to Do

Help Nora get from the Island of Mean to the Land of True Popularity.

... And More to Do!

Think of three truly popular kids you know. What do you think makes them so popular?

____

____

____

____

What do they have in common?

____

____

____

____

How are they different from one another?

____

____

____

____

Your Social Network

Activity 7

For You to Know

Your social network is made up of the kids you know—your close friends, your acquaintances, and the friends of your friends. The more kids you already know, the more kids you can get to know.

Reaching out to new kids can be scary. Even grown-ups sometimes feel nervous when they are meeting new people. That's normal.

It can help to remember that there is something special about each person you meet. They may be a lot like you, a little like you, or very different from you. But every one of them is like a whole new world for you to learn about.

For You to Do

Write your name in the circle. Then write the names of six kids in your social network who are important to you. Below each name, list one talent, strength, or quality this person has that expands your world.

Name: ____________________

____

Name: ____________________

____

Name: ____________________

____

Name: ____________________

____

Name: ____________________

____

Name: ____________________

____

... And More to Do!

What are some of the different skills kids in your social network have?

____

____

____

Tell about a time when someone asked you for help with a problem they knew you would be able to solve.

____

____

____

Tell about a time when you asked someone in your social network for their special help.

____

____

____

Activity 8 Reaching Out to New Kids

For You to Know

One great way to try starting a friendship is to invite another kid to spend time with you outside of school. You might play a sport, watch a movie, or work on a project together. Even if you are worried that this person already has other plans or won't think that your plan sounds like fun, try anyway. You will be letting this kid know that you want to be friends.

Morgan had just moved to a new neighborhood. She still saw her old friends on the weekends and had lots of fun with them. But at her new school she was often lonely and felt like she didn't belong. Her older sister said, "The other kids aren't mind readers. How can they tell that you want to be friends if you don't let them know?"

Morgan thought she would like to be friends with Maria, a girl in her gym class. Maria seemed kind. She was a good basketball player and never minded when other kids asked for help. She seemed friendly, too. Morgan remembered that Maria had made a point of saying hello when she first came to school.

There was a basketball hoop at Morgan's new house. After gym class one day, she thought about what her sister had said, and walked up to Maria. She smiled and said, "That was a great shot you made."

"Oh, thank you!" said Maria, smiling back.

"I just got a new basketball for my birthday," said Morgan. "Would you like to come over on Saturday? We could shoot hoops."

For You to Do

Here are some possible answers Maria might give. On the line below each, write what Morgan might say.

If Maria says, "Saturday afternoon is great! I'd love to come."

Morgan could say:

____

____

If Maria says, "I have to go to my aunt's house on Saturday. I can't make it."

Morgan could say:

____

____

If Maria says, "I already have basketball practice on Saturday morning, but thanks anyway."

Morgan could say:

____

____

... And More to Do!

Tell about a time when someone tried to start a friendship with you.

How did you react?

Tell about a time when you invited someone new to do something with you.

How did that person react to your invitation?

Section II: Understanding Social Rules

Do you think rules are a good thing? Lots of kids say they don't like rules, but rules are very important in getting along with other people.

Imagine there were no rules about how to behave at the dinner table. People would grab food, eat with their hands, burp, and do all kinds of other gross things. The biggest people might grab all the food and not leave much for the smallest people.

Imagine there were no traffic rules. Drivers would go as fast as they wanted to, no one would know what to do at an intersection, and there would be lots of accidents.

Now imagine there were no social rules. People wouldn't say please or thank you, or even hello or good-bye. Everyone would just do whatever they wanted, and it would be very crazy. Even animals need social rules. Have you ever watched a flock of birds or a group of monkeys at the zoo? These animals can't talk, but they still have social rules they need to follow to get along.

This section will teach you about social rules for getting along with kids. You already know some of these rules, and others may be new for you. The more you understand about social rules, the easier it will be for you to make and keep good friends.

Activity 9 Being a Social Detective

For You to Know

Watching other kids can help you learn how to act so that others will want to be friends with you. It can also show you what behavior is likely to make kids avoid you.

Being a social detective doesn't mean hiding around corners and spying on people from a distance. It means paying attention to how people act in different situations. It also means watching what effect their actions have on other people. What happens when the checkout person at the supermarket is always grumpy, for instance? What happens when one kid refuses again and again to share with other kids? What happens when someone is often friendly or helpful to other people?

For You to Do

Be a detective for a day by watching how people affect situations with their behavior. You can make your observations at school, at home, or when you are out, perhaps at a store or the library. Then write down four things you observed. (The first row is an example.)

Who Did It	What Happened First	What Happened Next
A boy on the school bus	He smiled at the new kid.	Both kids started talking to each other.

... And More to Do!

Tell about a time when something you did or said changed a situation.

What kinds of behavior seem to work best when dealing with other people?

Which behaviors work less well?

For You to Know

When kids are trying to form a group, finding out what they have in common is the first step.

People in a group usually care about one another and want to be with each other. They probably spend lots of time together. But what keeps a group together is most often what they have in common. Common ground can be something very specific, such as a group of dog lovers who meet at the local dog run. It can be something simple, like having the same teacher at school, or it can be something broader, like finding the same jokes funny.

For You to Do

Below are three gardens. Eric has already planted his, and the other two are ready to be planted. Looking at the labels in Eric's garden, you can see what he has in common with his group. In the garden labeled "My Family," plant some things that you and your family members have in common. In the garden labeled "My Friends," plant some of the talents, interests, or skills you have in common with your friends.

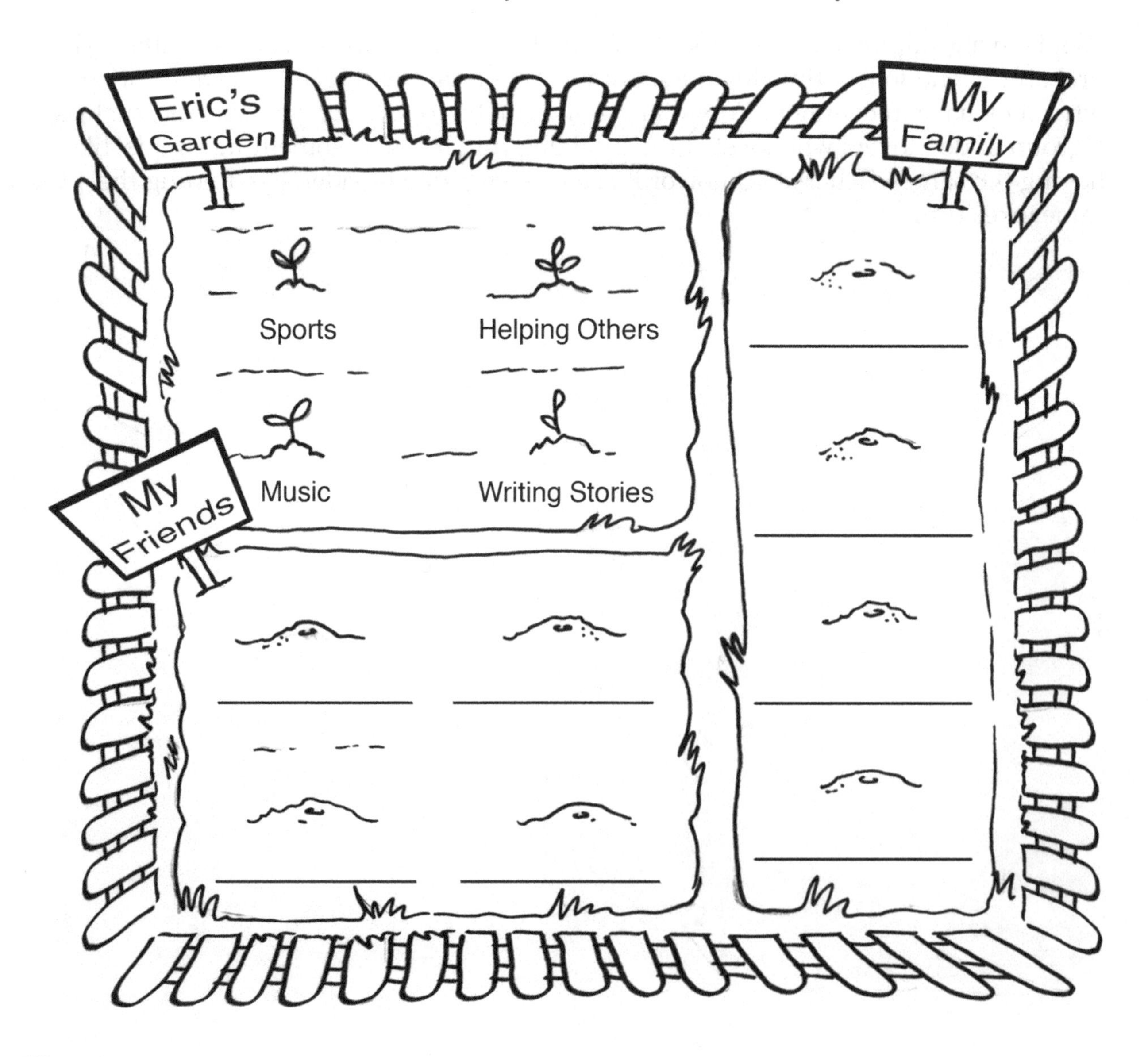

... *And More to Do!*

Why do think common interests are important to your friendships?

____

____

____

____

Which of the things you wrote down is most important to you?

____

____

____

____

Activity 11 Finding the Right Words

For You to Know

Your words can help somebody feel better or worse, and how you express yourself affects whether other kids will want to be friendly with you.

Jake didn't mind doing things by himself, but everything was more fun with his best buddies, Shawn and Reed. One Saturday morning, Jake wanted to ride his bike to the skateboard park with his friends. He put on his helmet, strapped his skateboard to the back of his bike, and headed over to Shawn's house. He rang the bell, and Shawn answered the door, holding a bag of ice to his head.

"Do you want to go skateboarding?" Jake asked with a smile. "Get your bike and let's go!"

"No, not now," Shawn said slowly, with a look of pain.

"Okay," Jake said, "maybe later." He got back on his bike and rode over to Reed's house. When he got there, the door was open, so he walked right in. He saw Reed eating breakfast with his little brother. They were both still in their pajamas.

"Do you want to go skateboarding?" Jake asked.

"Not right now," Reed said. "We're still eating our—" But Jake didn't wait for Reed to finish his sentence. "Okay, then," he said, "maybe later."

Later that afternoon, Jake rode over to the playground, and he was shocked at what he saw. Shawn and Reed were there, playing! He went up to them and said, "Hey, I thought you guys were busy. When I came to get you earlier, you didn't want to come with me!"

"I did want to come with you," Shawn said, "but I had just fallen and hurt myself. Didn't you see I had an icepack on my head? You didn't even ask what happened."

"I wanted to come too," Reed said, "but didn't you see I was still eating breakfast? You didn't give me a chance to ask you to wait."

"I'm sorry, guys," Jake said, and he took a deep breath. "Can I play with you now?" And that was the smartest thing Jake had said all day.

For You to Do

Jon always tries to find the right words. Below each of the following scenes, write what Jon could say.

... And More to Do!

Tell about a time when it was hard for you to find the right words.

____

____

____

____

What made it so difficult to know what to say?

____

____

____

Tell about a time when you knew just what to say.

____

____

____

____

What made it so easy?

____

____

____

Activity 12 Understanding Body Language

For You to Know

Words are not the only way we communicate. Our bodies have their own language that often says as much—or more—about what we are feeling than our words do. Sometimes our body language sends a message that is the same as our actual words; sometimes it sends a different message.

Have you ever been speaking to someone and thought, "She says she's happy, but she sure doesn't seem it." Maybe you have had your feelings hurt by someone who says he is listening, but keeps looking around the room as you talk.

Being aware of your body language is as important as being aware of your words. Imagine you are trying to apologize for something you've done. If you cross your arms and frown and say, "Sorry!" through clenched teeth, the odds are that people won't consider that a real apology.

Human beings are natural social detectives, and we read one another's body language easily. Real detectives even use body language to help determine if people are telling the truth—people may say one thing but show their nervousness by blinking their eyes or failing to make eye contact.

For You to Do

Are you a body language expert? Below each picture, write what you think the person is feeling.

... And More to Do!

What body language tells someone that you are:

Tired?

____

____

Interested?

____

____

Afraid?

____

____

Relaxed?

____

____

For You to Know

Having good manners lets other people know that you care about them. When you use good manners with others, they will probably use good manners with you.

The NewBot 3000 is an amazing robot. It can lift things ten times its size, run as fast as a train, and solve hundreds of math problems in just minutes. Its main mission in life is to help people.

There is just one problem. The NewBot hasn't been programmed with good manners, so it is constantly running into trouble. Even the people it tries to help don't want anything to do with this rude robot.

For You to Do

On the lines below, list five things NewBot 3000 can do to show others that it has good manners.

... And More to Do!

Why are good manners important?

___

___

___

Think of someone you know who has good manners. What are three things that person does that show good manners?

___

___

___

What effect do good manners have on others?

___

___

___

Activity 14 Phone Manners

For You to Know

There are special social rules for getting to know people over the telephone, calling friends' houses, and answering the phone.

On the phone, you can't see the kids you are talking to, so it's impossible to read their body language or for them to read yours. You can't communicate friendliness by making eye contact or smiling, but you can communicate friendliness by following these simple rules:

1. Use a friendly voice.
2. Listen carefully.
3. Wait your turn to speak.

For You to Do

Joaquim and Jenna are next-door neighbors. During the summer, they like to set up an old-fashioned telephone using string and two cups. One afternoon, Joaquim wasn't paying close attention to their conversation, and Jenna's feelings were hurt. Use the blank lines in the column on the right to rewrite Joaquim's responses.

Jenna: Hi.

Joaquim: Hey.

Jenna: How are you?

Joaquim: I'm all right. It's hot.

Jenna: Yeah, it is pretty hot today. What are you going to do?

Joaquim: I don't know. Maybe go swimming with my brother, maybe go to the library.

Jenna: I think I'll just stay home today.

Joaquim: Sounds good.

Jenna: Yeah, I guess I just don't feel like going out.

Joaquim: [silence]

Jenna: Hello?

Joaquim: Sorry, I got distracted.

Jenna: You're probably the only person I feel like talking to anyway.

Joaquim: Cool. Hey, my brother just got home, so I gotta go.

Jenna: Fine.

Joaquim: See you later.

Jenna: Hi.

Joaquim: Hey.

Jenna: How are you?

Joaquim: I'm all right. It's hot.

Jenna: Yeah, it is pretty hot today. What are you going to do?

Joaquim: I don't know. Maybe go swimming with my brother, maybe go to the library.

Jenna: I think I'll just stay home today.

Joaquim: Sounds good.

Jenna: ______________________________

Joaquim: ______________________________

Jenna: ______________________________

Joaquim: ______________________________

Jenna: ______________________________

Joaquim: ______________________________

Jenna: ______________________________

Joaquim: ______________________________

… And More to Do!

What do you say when you answer the phone?

____

____

What do you say when you call a friend's house and a parent answers?

____

____

How do you end a phone call?

____

____

E-Mail Manners

For You to Know

E-mail can be an easy way to communicate with friends, but even when you are sending an e-mail, you should be polite.

It's important to pay as much attention to writing e-mail as you would if you were writing a letter or having a conversation with someone. Pay special attention to how you begin and end your e-mail. Depending on how well you know the person, you might sign off with "Sincerely" or "See you soon." Before you send it, read over what you have written. If you think the other person might misunderstand what you are trying to say, rewrite your e-mail.

For You to Do

In the space below, write an e-mail to someone you admire. You can write to a family member, friend, or teacher, or someone you don't know personally, such as a writer, musician, or scientist whose work you think a lot of.

... And More to Do!

How is e-mail different from speaking to someone face to face or over the phone?

____

____

____

____

How is e-mail the same?

____

____

____

____

Do you think it is easier to talk to people face to face or by e-mail? Tell why.

____

____

____

____

Activity 16 Planning a Party

For You to Know

Parties are a fun way to bring kids together. Planning in advance makes it more likely that your friends will have a good time and that you will have a good time as well!

Hannah wanted to plan her birthday party all by herself. Her parents thought that was a great idea, and they asked Hannah to think about what she could do make sure the party would go well. She asked her friend Danielle to help her plan. Together, Hannah and Danielle came up with these ideas:

1. Ask my parents how many kids I can invite.
2. Make up a guest list.
3. Send out my invitations at least two weeks before the party.
4. Choose at least three activities to do at the party.
5. Serve food that most kids will like, but have some other choices available.

Hannah's parents said she should plan to do one more thing: have fun at the party herself!

For You to Do

Think of each of the dots below as a kid at your party. Bring them all together by connecting the dots to complete the picture.

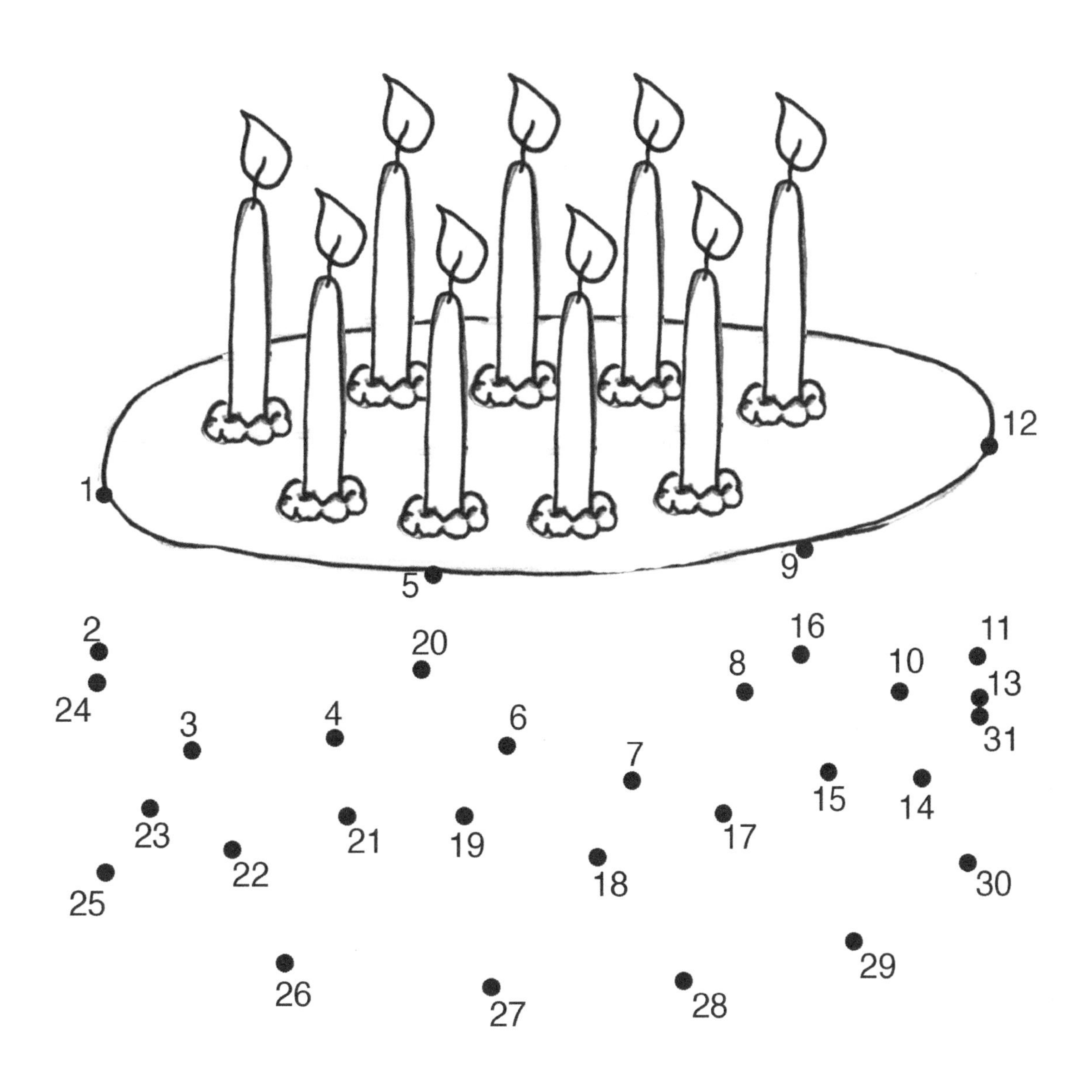

... And More to Do!

What are some ways you can bring kids together at a party?

Why is it important to have a good time at your own party?

Think about parties you have gone to that were the most fun. What made them fun?

Section III: The Give and Take of Friendships

Being a good friend can take some work, but it is a fun kind of work. Good friends are always learning about each other, every single day. Sometimes you learn things that mean you have to change your behavior. The activities in this section will help you think about some things you might want to change and some things you might want your friends to do differently.

Friendship can be a lot like playing on a seesaw. When one person goes up, the other goes down. Then you switch roles. You can't really seesaw if you don't take your turn at the right time and pay attention to the person you are with. And what would happen if you tried to seesaw by yourself? You wouldn't go very far.

Activity 17 Share and Share Alike

For You to Know

Sharing is an important part of being a friend. It is a good way to show others that you care about them.

All social groups—from small groups of friends to whole communities—rely on sharing things. Kids share books and toys. They share ideas and information. They share their time when they help others. They even share their friends with each other.

There are many different ways to share, and each of them can help you build friendships. It isn't always easy to share, but you can become better at it if you ask yourself this question: would I rather be friends with someone who shares or someone who is selfish?

For You to Do

On the lines below, use the left-hand column to make a list of six things that you care a lot about. Look over your list and put a 1 next to the thing that would be easiest to share, a 2 next to the thing that would be second easiest, and so on. Put the number 6 next to the thing you would find hardest to share.

____________________ ____________________

____________________ ____________________

____________________ ____________________

____________________ ____________________

____________________ ____________________

____________________ ____________________

In the right-hand column, write the name of someone you would be happy to share it with. You can write the same name on as many lines as you like.

... And More to Do!

What kind of person are you most likely to want to share with?

Is there anything on the list that you would have a hard time sharing with anyone? If so, tell why it would be difficult to share this thing.

How do you feel when people share with you?

How do you feel when you share with other people?

Taking Turns — Activity 18

For You to Know

It can be hard to wait your turn when you're very excited to be a part of something, but it's important. Taking turns allows everyone to have fun. It makes whatever you are trying to do go more smoothly.

Ahmed, Ben, and Kevin were at Ahmed's house, trying to make plans for the afternoon.

Ahmed said, "I think we should—"

In a loud voice, Ben said, "I know! We could—"

And at the same time, Kevin said, "I've got a great idea. Let's—" His voice was loudest of all.

Each boy had an idea of what he wanted to do, and they each wanted to be the first to tell about their idea. None of them would let the others have a turn to talk. Their voices grew so loud that finally Ahmed said, "Wait! Let's spend the afternoon having fun, not shouting. If we each take a turn to talk, we can decide together what we want do."

For You to Do

Can you help Ahmed, Ben, and Kevin take turns and make sense of their conversation? Unscramble the letters to spell fun activities. The answers are upside down at the bottom of the page.

Answers: movie; park; soccer; museum; board game; fun run

... And More to Do!

Can you think of four other times when people have to take turns?

1. ______________________________

2. ______________________________

3. ______________________________

4. ______________________________

Choose one of these situations and tell what would happen if someone did not wait for a turn.

____

____

____

____

Tell about a time when someone cut in line or refused to wait their turn. How did it make you feel?

____

____

____

____

Activity 19 Tuning In

For You to Know

Listening carefully is one of the best ways to show other kids that you care about what they have to say. When you listen closely to them, people are more likely to listen closely to you.

Listening to each other is another way to take turns. Most kids can tell right away when someone isn't paying attention to what they are saying.

How do you know when kids are listening to you? They usually make eye contact and seem interested. They ask questions about the things you've said. After you have finished speaking, they remember what you've told them.

For You to Do

Good reporters are excellent listeners. They listen carefully, ask good questions, and remember what they've heard. Find a friend or family member and ask them to tell you about themselves—how they are, something they've done recently, or whatever they'd like to talk about. Pay close attention to the person you're interviewing, but don't take notes. Just listen carefully, and be sure to ask good questions that get them to say more.

When you're done, fill in this person's name in the title at the top of the next page, and write what you found out by listening.

What I Learned About ______________________________

What I Learned About ______________________________

... And More to Do!

How do you feel when someone listens closely to you?

____

How do you feel when someone doesn't pay careful attention to what you are saying?

____

Did you find it easy or hard to remember what the person you interviewed said?

____

What could you do to be an even better listener next time?

____

____

____

For You to Know

Giving sincere compliments is a sure way to make other kids feel good, and it can also make you feel great!

What you say to others has a big impact on them. If you give someone a genuine compliment about something they have accomplished, something they do well, or something they've been trying hard to change, you can make them feel good for the rest of the day.

Sometimes giving a compliment can be tricky. Imagine you have a shy friend who is trying out for the school play and comes to you for encouragement. Even if you don't think your friend is a great actor, you can still find something to compliment. You might simply compliment your friend for being brave enough to try something new.

For You to Do

For each of these situations, write a compliment you could give sincerely.

A friend has just gotten a good haircut.

____

____

Your sister won first prize in the science fair.

____

____

Your mom tried a new recipe for your birthday dinner. You know how hard she worked, but you don't like it.

____

____

A classmate who has never tried writing a poem before has decided to enter the school poetry competition. He's worried about what others will think of his poem.

____

____

A family member has been trying to get in shape by starting an exercise program and is losing steam after a week.

____

____

... And More to Do!

Think of a sincere compliment someone has given you that made you feel especially good. Why was this compliment particularly important to you?

____

____

____

What made you feel that the compliment was sincere?

____

____

____

Activity 21 Being a Good Leader

For You to Know

When a group needs a leader or when you are uncomfortable with what others in a group are doing, it's time to step up and lead.

Being a good leader is a lot of responsibility, and it can be very hard. You have to know where you're headed and have confidence in your ability to lead others there. All good leaders listen carefully to others before making a decision.

You may find yourself in a situation where one kid, or a small group of kids, is making all the decisions for the group. If you want to propose a different idea, you'll have to persuade people to follow you.

For You to Do

These eight words describe the qualities a good leader should have. Can you find them in the word search below?

A good leader is …

WISE	CAREFUL
DECISIVE	HELPFUL
ATTENTIVE	CONFIDENT
GENEROUS	HONEST

E	J	U	K	P	C	O	N	F	I	D	E	N	T	V	R
C	P	B	E	F	N	N	M	G	W	C	X	L	K	Y	J
R	A	M	L	E	M	P	L	T	L	W	P	L	Q	Y	A
E	A	R	K	F	N	O	K	G	O	I	O	K	A	H	E
E	S	L	E	V	B	I	J	F	U	S	I	J	Z	N	H
P	D	P	J	F	V	Y	H	V	T	E	U	J	X	M	U
K	G	K	G	A	U	L	F	N	W	H	T	G	W	H	F
U	H	N	F	Y	C	L	D	H	S	R	R	F	E	O	A
Y	J	I	D	U	X	T	S	U	D	E	E	D	D	N	T
T	K	N	S	I	Z	R	A	J	F	S	W	S	C	E	T
H	L	D	E	C	I	S	I	V	E	F	Q	A	V	S	E
E	Q	U	S	P	S	E	A	E	U	F	A	A	F	T	N
L	W	H	P	L	D	W	S	S	H	K	S	I	R	U	T
P	E	B	O	N	F	Q	E	X	N	H	D	U	T	I	I
F	R	Y	I	N	G	A	D	Z	G	E	F	Y	G	K	V
U	T	G	U	F	H	S	R	A	R	E	F	R	B	L	E
L	Y	V	Y	R	J	G	E	N	E	R	O	U	S	O	Q
D	U	T	T	D	L	D	T	O	R	C	G	R	T	P	P

... And More to Do!

List three leaders you admire. You can name public figures, such as community leaders, or people in your own family or group of friends.

1. ______________________________

2. ______________________________

3. ______________________________

Tell about a time when one of these leaders showed some of the qualities you found that were hidden in the word search.

____

____

____

Which quality do you think is most important to good leadership? Tell why.

____

____

____

Knowing When to Follow   Activity 22

For You to Know

In different situations, each of us is sometimes a follower and sometimes a leader. The trick is to know when and whom to follow.

David, Cassie, Lisa, and Han were all on a summer camping trip with their families. While their parents relaxed at the campsite, the four friends decided to go on a short hike through the nearby woods.

After wandering along happily for a while, they reached a crossroads. They realized that they didn't know which trail they had started on and weren't sure how to get back to the campsite. Everyone had a different idea about what to do. David suggested they try the blue trail, Cassie the orange trail, and Lisa the yellow trail.

Han was quiet while the others talked. Finally he said, "I'm sure it's the white trail. I remember that the white markers looked like snow on the tree branches, and I wondered what it would be like to go camping here in the winter." David, Cassie, and Lisa all thought that Han's reason made sense, and they knew that he usually made thoughtful decisions, so they stopped arguing. They followed him down the white trail and got safely back to camp.

For You to Do

Read the situations below. Put a check mark next to the ones in which following the group plan seems like a good idea. Put an X next to the ones in which it is better not to follow the group.

______ A friend has organized a game of soccer in the park after school. You always play the goalie, and it's your favorite position. This time, your friend insists on playing goalie and asks you to play forward.

______ Some girls tell you that they've been sending mean e-mails to the new kid in your class. They want you to join them.

______ A classmate has started a band and asks you to join when the regular drummer drops out. You like the other band members and you are happy to have kids to play with, but you aren't crazy about the kind of music they play.

______ Some kids at school have organized a math study group and invited you to come. You are worried that other kids will make fun of you, but you could really use the help in math.

______ You and several other kids are hanging out with a friend at his house. Everyone is having fun just being together when your friend suggests playing a mean trick on his little brother. The other kids all seem willing to go along with the trick.

... And More to Do!

What do you find easiest about following others?

____

____

____

How is following others sometimes a difficult or complicated thing to do?

____

____

____

Tell about a time you decided to go along with a group. What happened?

____

____

____

Activity 23 Making the Best of Things

For You to Know

Being able to make the best of situations is a good way to have more fun. It's important to remember that small things always pass. The big picture is what matters. Learning how to keep your eye on it—even when you are upset by something like an argument with a friend, a disappointment, or a mistake—can help you feel happier.

Everyone feels disappointed when an exciting plan doesn't work out for one reason or another. But it's important to look beyond that disappointment and to think of new, fun possibilities. Let's say you had planned to go the park on Saturday to play soccer with your friends. All Saturday morning the sky is gray, with big, dark clouds rolling in, and your mood also grows darker and darker by the hour. When the rain starts, you might be upset or feel like losing your temper. That's understandable, but you have to remember the big picture—you still have a whole Saturday to do something else you enjoy.

For You to Do

The kids in these pictures are disappointed because their plans have changed. Can you help them change their thoughts into more optimistic ones?

This rain is ruining the whole weekend!

____

____

____

Lee said he would draw with me today, and now he's helping someone else!

____

____

____

Mom promised we would go to the bookstore this afternoon, but now she says she doesn't have time.

____

____

____

I wish Jen was here. There's nothing to do without her.

____

____

____

... *And More to Do!*

Tell about a time when you did something fun on a rainy day.

____

____

____

____

Was there ever a time when you didn't want to do something at first and ended up having more fun than you expected? Tell what happened.

____

____

____

____

Activity 24 Being Flexible

For You to Know

People sometimes have to change their plans. Once you get past being disappointed, you may find that a change of plans ends up leading to something even better.

It was the first day of summer vacation, and Halima couldn't wait to go to the local pool. She was excited about swimming again, but she was even more excited about spending the day with her two best friends, Carlos and Elizabeth.

It seemed like the perfect day until things started to go wrong. First, Halima's mother said they would have to wait at the house for a delivery. Halima rolled her eyes, stamped her foot, and said, "But I don't want to wait! Carlos and Elizabeth will already be at the pool." Halima's mother reminded her that she would only be able to go to the pool if she was well behaved. Halima tried hard to make herself feel better. She reminded herself that this was just a little delay, and she would be swimming soon enough.

After the delivery finally arrived, Halima and her mother walked to the pool. At the entrance, they found a big sign that said "Closed for Repairs." Halima couldn't believe her terrible luck. All she could think about was how the whole day was ruined. The whole summer might be ruined!

Her mother said, "I'm sure the pool will open in the next couple of weeks. Why don't you call Carlos and Elizabeth to see what they're doing?" Halima thought about her mother's suggestion and decided that it was a good idea—she would call Carlos and Elizabeth and see if they wanted to come over for the day. They always had fun together, pool or no pool. With a new plan, Halima felt calmer.

For You to Do

Draw a picture that shows something fun Halima, Carlos, and Elizabeth could do instead of going swimming.

... And More to Do!

Tell about a time when you were looking forward to plans that changed at the last minute. How did you feel?

____

____

____

____

Do you find it easy or hard to adjust to a new plan? Tell why.

____

____

____

____

Can you think of a time when you were able to adjust to a new plan? Tell what happened.

____

____

____

____

Speaking Kindly Activity 25

For You to Know

What you say to other kids has a big effect on them, so it's important to try to say things kindly. There are even times when it's a good idea not to say anything at all.

Unkind words or critical remarks stick with other people for a long time after you have said them. Even if kids don't react right away, you can bet that they will continue to be hurt by them. If you are worried about the way someone does something, think before you speak. How can you talk about this problem without hurting their feelings? Are you sure that your criticism is fair—is it something that they need to change for their own good, or is it something they truly can't help about themselves?

For You to Do

Read these situations and then tell what each kid could say to be kind and helpful. If you think it would be better not to say anything, tell why.

Ever since Jorge's older brother broke up with his girlfriend, he has been very blue. He just lies around all afternoon, watching television and eating junk food, and he sleeps a lot. Jorge understands why his brother is sad, but it's been a month since the break-up, and now his brother is out of shape and cranky and he refuses to do anything fun.

What could Jorge say to his brother?

____

____

____

____

Michael always looks forward to seeing his mother when she comes home from work. He helps her cook dinner, and she helps him with homework. They sometimes pack lunch together for the next day or play a board game before Michael has to go to bed. On Wednesdays and Fridays, his mother has to work a double shift. When she comes home on those nights, she is tired and irritable. She doesn't want to do anything together and she seems distracted whenever Michael tries to tell her about his day at school. When she acts that way, his feelings are hurt.

What could Michael say to his mother?

____

____

____

____

Sarah and Vanessa have been friends since first grade. They hang out every day at school and on most weekends. They like the same music and the same books, and they have the same taste in clothes. They are both popular at school, play lots of sports, and like to be with people. One day, Sarah announced that she was giving up basketball and joining the school's poetry club. Vanessa was baffled—they had always done things together, and suddenly Sarah was going off in a new direction. Didn't she realize how much it would change their lives if she started hanging out with the poetry kids instead of the basketball team?

What could Vanessa say to Sarah?

____

____

____

____

... And More to Do!

Can you think of a time when someone said something critical to you? Tell what happened.

How did it make you feel about yourself?

How did it make you feel about the person who said those things?

Keeping Cool

For You to Know

Everyone gets angry at times, but you can learn to manage how you show your anger. When you keep cool, it is more likely that you will be able to cope with what made you feel angry.

Eddie the Volcano can't help blowing his top sometimes. After all, he is a volcano. But even volcanoes must learn to control their tempers if they want to spend time around others. Eddie's little brother has just accidentally broken his favorite CD. Eddie can feel himself getting angrier and angrier.

For You to Do

Color the deepest level of the volcano with a fiery color. On the line next to it, write how you feel when you're angriest. Then color the next level up with a slightly cooler color, like light orange. On the line next to it, write your first tip to Eddie: something he can do to start calming down. Do the same in the third section, and so on, each time giving Eddie helpful hints for feeling calm, and coloring in cooler and cooler colors as you go.

... And More to Do!

How can you tell when you are losing your temper?

____

____

____

How does your voice change?

____

____

How do you hold your body?

____

____

In addition to the advice you gave Eddie, can you think of anything else that helps you keep your temper cool?

____

____

____

Activity 27 Releasing Your Feelings

For You to Know

When you pretend things don't bother you, they have a way of building up in your mind—and then bothering you more and more. But talking about your feelings will help you feel better, and it will also help your friends understand you better.

Emily was really angry at her best friend, Brooke. She had overheard Brooke telling some other girls that Emily was spoiled. "Why would she say I'm spoiled?" Emily asked her mother. "I don't act spoiled. I think Brooke is just jealous of my new clothes."

"I don't know if that's true," Emily's mother said. "Why don't you ask her why she thinks you are spoiled?"

"I can't do that!" Emily told her mother. "She'll think I was spying on her."

"You weren't spying," her mother said. "You just overheard her talking, and you can't help that. But it sounds like you feel angry and hurt. What will happen if you don't tell Brooke about your feelings?"

Emily thought about that. "Well, I guess she won't know my feelings are hurt. And I guess I'll stay mad. And I guess we won't be friends anymore."

"Is that what you want to happen?" Emily's mother asked.

"Not at all," Emily said, and she picked up the phone to call Brooke.

For You to Do

In the jar below, make a list of feelings you sometimes keep from other people.

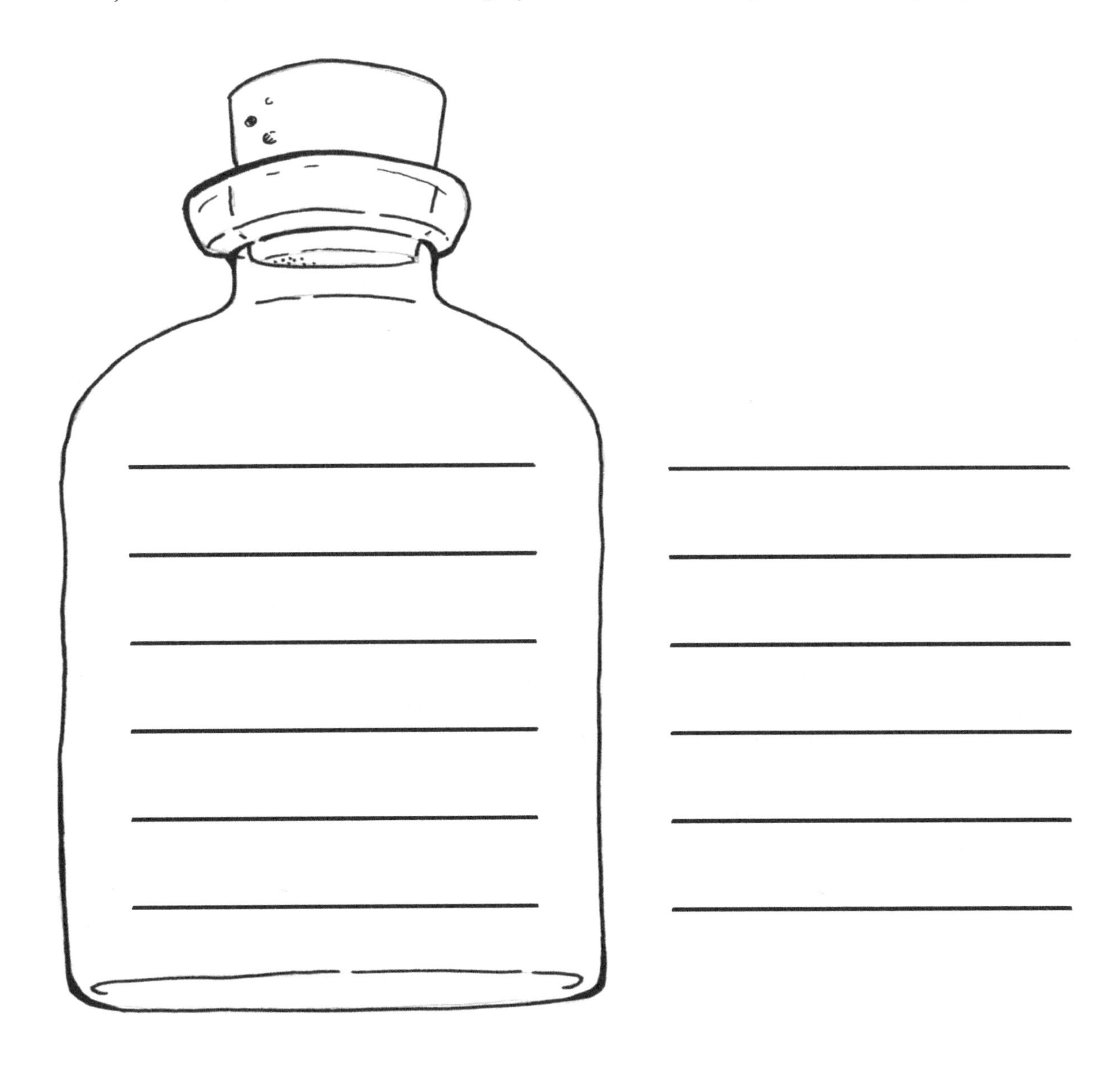

Now take each feeling you listed. On the lines outside the jar, write how or with whom you could have shared your feeling.

... And More to Do!

What makes you keep some feelings to yourself?

Have you ever been angry and thought it was better not to talk about it? What happened?

When you hold your feelings in, sometimes your body starts to talk back to you. You may get headaches or stomachaches or have trouble sleeping. Has something like this ever happened to you? Tell what happened.

Bouncing Back from Rejection

For You to Know

Even though being rejected may make you feel bad, you can get over it and bounce back to feeling good.

Rejection is a part of life for everyone, not just for kids, but for grown-ups, too. It may be hard to believe, but being rejected can teach you something. It can help you think about what you believe in and what is really important to you.

Here's the secret to coping with rejection: learn from what happened, put it behind you, and go on to make new friends.

For You to Do

Think of a time when you felt rejected by someone else and your feelings were hurt. In the space below, write a short letter to yourself, explaining what happened, how you felt, and how everything turned out in the end.

What did you learn from the experience?

____

____

____

____

If something like this happened again, what could you do?

____

____

____

____

... And More to Do!

Tell about a time when you may have made someone feel rejected, either on purpose or accidentally.

____

____

____

____

How did you feel right afterward?

____

____

____

____

How do you feel when you think about it now?

____

____

____

____

Section IV:
Understanding and Caring About Your Friends

Understanding what other people are feeling is called "empathy." Some kids find it easy to empathize with others, and they are very sensitive to what their friends are feeling. Other kids find it hard to empathize with their friends. They say and do whatever they feel like, and they don't really think about how it affects others.

Caring and empathy go hand in hand. The more you show that you care about your friends, the more they will feel like you understand them. You will never go wrong when you show your friends that you care.

Activity 29 Paying Attention to Feelings

For You to Know

Even without thinking about it, people often sense what those around them are feeling. Before you have a chance to think, "My best friend seems sad today" or "Mom is in a great mood," you might just suddenly feel a bit blue or a bit more cheerful around them.

When you're talking to other kids, it's important to pay attention to how they're feeling. You can do this by listening carefully and watching their body language, and also by paying attention to your own feelings. If it seems to you like things are okay, they probably are. But if you feel like something is wrong, something probably *is* wrong.

It is easier to be aware of people's feelings when everything is calm, but very often people are in a hurry—especially grown-ups. They may be rushing from home to work. They may be rushing to finish their errands or to get everything done by the end of the day. At busy times, it may be harder to pick up on the subtle clues to someone's mood.

For You to Do

Without drawing attention to yourself, observe three people over the course of the day. Try to detect what they are really feeling, regardless of what they say or do. You don't need to speak to them directly. Just be close enough to hear what they are saying and to observe their body language.

Subject #1

How did this person seem at first glance?

____

____

How do you think this person really felt?

____

____

What clues led you to this conclusion?

____

____

Subject #2

How did this person seem at first glance?

____

____

How do you think this person really felt?

____

____

What clues led you to this conclusion?

____

____

Subject #3

How did this person seem at first glance?

____

____

How do you think this person really felt?

____

____

What clues led you to this conclusion?

____

____

... And More to Do!

Think of a close friend or family member. How do you know when this person is angry?

____

____

____

How do you know when this person is in an especially good mood?

____

____

____

How do you know when this person is sad?

____

____

____

Activity 30 Helping Others

For You to Know

Helping others is important, and it is also easy. You can even find chances to help people before they ask for it.

Brandon called his friend Josh and said, "Let's ride bikes." Josh said, "I can't. I have to clean up my room before I can go out." So Brandon offered to help Josh, and pretty soon, the boys were riding their bikes.

Rachel noticed that her friend Jessica looked very upset. "What's wrong?" she asked. Jessica said, "I'm having a really hard time with this art project." Rachel said, "I'll help you." Their art teacher saw Rachel sharing ideas with Jessica, and she gave Rachel a big smile. So did Jessica!

James was new in school, and he had forgotten where his locker was. Andrew saw that he looked confused and asked if he could help. James said, "I can't find my locker," and Andrew offered to walk him there. On the way, they talked about sports and found out that they both had the same favorite player.

Brandon, Rachel, and Andrew all knew that helping others is a good way to make and keep friends.

For You to Do

Complete the bridge by filling in the blank stones with examples of big and small ways in which you've helped others.

... *And More to Do!*

Tell about three ways other people have helped you.

____

____

____

How do you feel when others help you? ______________________

How do you feel when you help others? ______________________

Who is the most helpful kid you know? ______________________

Tell about a time this kid was helpful.

____

____

____

Being Too Nice

For You to Know

You've been thinking a lot about how to be as kind and helpful to others as possible, but, believe it or not, it's possible to be *too* nice.

Alex was always eager to help people. His mother suggested that he try to think about being too nice. She told him to ask himself whether someone really needed his help or was just taking advantage of his good nature.

The best way to avoid being too nice is to pay attention to how other kids act toward you. Are they returning favors that you do for them? If you offer them help, do they offer help to you? Do they seem to appreciate your kindness, or do they seem disinterested, or even annoyed, by your efforts to be nice?

For You to Do

Read the examples below. Then write three more examples of good helping on the left. On the right, write three examples of helping that is too nice.

Good Helping	Being Too Nice
Alex's little brother asks Alex for help with his math homework.	A classmate asks Alex to do his math homework for him.

... And More to Do!

Who is the nicest person you know? ______________________________

Tell about a time this person was a good helper.

____

____

____

Tell about someone you know who is too nice.

____

____

____

Why might being too nice become a problem?

____

____

____

Activity 32 Including Everyone

For You to Know

Most kids want to spend time with a group of their close friends, or even with one special friend, but it's important not to exclude others in the process. Excluding other people is a way of rejecting them, which we know makes people very unhappy. Friendships are a two-way street—if you include people in your plans, the chances are that they will include you in theirs.

Brian loved to play basketball, and he was really good at it. He was great at dribbling and passing and, of course, shooting baskets. He was such a good player that he started to play with kids who were one or two or even three years older. And he would still often be the best player on the court!

But when the game was over, the other kids would hang out together, and they wouldn't invite Brian to come along. They would get on their bikes and leave Brian standing by himself on the basketball court. Although he wanted to hang out with them, Brian felt too shy to say anything, so he just went home.

One day after a basketball game, Brian was feeling particularly lonely. The older boys were going out for ice cream, and they hadn't asked him to come along. He shot baskets by himself for a while, and then he would just go home.

As soon as Brian got home, his younger brother Sam asked if he wanted to play. "Nah," Brian said, "you're too young to play with." Sam's feelings were hurt. He wanted to play with his older brother, but Brian never seemed to have time for him.

Sam and Brian each sat alone in their bedrooms, feeling sorry for themselves. They both felt that they had no one to be with.

Lots of kids are like Brian. They want to play only with one group of friends, and are unhappy when they are not included in this group. But they don't see that there are other kids at school, in their neighborhood, or even in their family who would love to have them for a playmate.

For You to Do

In each circle, write the names of kids you know who are close friends with each other. You can include yourself in any of these circles.

An exclusive group won't let anyone else join. Which of these groups is most exclusive? Outline the circle with a thick, dark line to show that it is hard to join this group. An inclusive group will let just about anyone join. Decide which of these groups is most inclusive and outline the circle with a thin line made up of little dots to show that it is easy for other people to join this group.

Now color the other circles thin or thick depending on how difficult it is to join these groups. Which group of friends do you think has the nicest people in it?

... *And More to Do!*

Tell about a time when you were excluded by others.

___

___

___

Can you think of a time that you excluded other kids? Tell what happened.

___

___

___

Why do you think it is a good idea for groups to be inclusive?

___

___

___

How do you think groups of friends can become more inclusive?

___

___

___

It's Nothing Personal Activity 33

For You to Know

We are all sensitive to the feelings of others, but it's important to remember that people's moods are caused by what is happening in their lives. If your friend is grumpy or your brother is angry, it probably has nothing to do with you.

Kids have all kinds of moods—and for all kinds of reasons. Sometimes when people don't even realize what is really upsetting them, they may act as if they are angry at the people close to them. It's hard not to get your feelings hurt when someone snaps at you, but before you start worrying—or snap back—think about what might be making that person angry.

For You to Do

Daniel was usually a nice guy, and he and Peter got along. Though they weren't close friends, Peter was happy when Daniel asked if they could work together on a science project.

Daniel wanted to make a volcano that erupted fake lava, but the teacher decided it would be too messy and told them to come up with a new idea. Peter suggested drawing a cross-section of a volcano and using paint to show how the lava reaches the surface. He was excited by this idea because he loved to paint and was a good artist. But Daniel gave him a cold look and said, "That's a stupid idea."

On the lines below, write three things that Peter might think without taking Daniel's comment personally.

1. ____

____

2. ____

____

3. ____

____

... And More to Do!

Think of someone you know who says hurtful things but doesn't mean to be unkind.

Why do you think this person does this?

____

____

____

How do you handle being around this person?

____

____

____

Activity 34 Forgiving Others

For You to Know

We all depend on others to forgive us when we have been selfish or hurtful in some way. Throughout life, you will ask your friends to forgive you and you will be asked to forgive others.

One Friday, Haley's teacher asked her to stay behind when the rest of the class left for lunch. "Is everything okay, Haley?" Ms. Slater asked. "You've seemed really upset all week."

Haley nearly burst into tears. "Everything's terrible! I thought Annie was my friend, but she had some kids sleep over last weekend, and I wasn't invited."

Ms. Slater said, "Did you talk to her about it?"

Haley said, "Yes. I told her that she had hurt my feelings. She said she didn't mean to, but she could have only a few girls, so she decided to invite kids she didn't usually get to hang out with. She said she was sorry my feelings were hurt, but I don't care. I'm still angry!"

Ms. Slater nodded. "I can see how angry you are, but you and Annie have been friends for a long time. You can choose to stay angry, or you can choose to forgive her. Which choice would make you feel better and let the two of you get back to having fun together?"

That afternoon, Haley called Annie and said, "It's okay. I know you didn't mean to hurt my feelings." Both girls were so relieved that Haley had forgiven Annie that they planned a sleepover to celebrate!

For You to Do

In the space below, write about a time when you were able to forgive someone who did something that seriously hurt your feelings. Be sure to include how you forgave that person. Did you forgive them in your thoughts, or did you actually tell the person that you forgave them?

... And More to Do!

Tell what made you decide to forgive this person.

What has happened in your relationship since you forgave that person?

Why do you think it is important to be a forgiving person?

Respecting Differences Activity 35

For You to Know

Differences make the world a better place. Even small differences between you and your friends make your time with them more interesting.

Most kids are alike in many ways. For example, they want others to like them, they want to do well, and they feel happier when things are going smoothly. And more often than not, friends get along with each other. But that doesn't mean they always agree or even that they have everything in common. There will always be differences—kids have different talents, experiences, and beliefs.

For You to Do

In the space below, write the names of three friends. List some ways in which you are different from each friend. Next, tell whether that difference matters to you. If it does, tell why.

Friend's Name	How We Are Different	Does This Difference Matter?
1.		
2.		
3.		

... And More to Do!

Are there any differences between you and a friend that you find hard to accept or to understand?

___

___

___

What is it about this difference that makes it hard to accept or understand?

___

___

___

How does this difference affect your friendship?

___

___

___

Section V: Peacemaking

Everyone has conflicts with their friends at some time. Almost every single day, you probably see kids and even adults disagree. There are different things that people do when they disagree. Some of these things are not very helpful, like arguing, sulking, calling someone names, or giving someone the silent treatment. But there are also positive ways to disagree and resolve differences, like compromising, seeing another person's point of view, and of course apologizing if you have done something wrong.

When you learn peacemaking skills, you can get along with just about anybody.

Activity 36 Dealing with Kids Who Are Difficult

For You to Know

We all have to deal with people we find difficult. Sometimes you may know why you find someone difficult. Maybe you don't like how this kid treats others or maybe you think this kid is mean. Sometimes you may simply feel like avoiding a particular kid without knowing exactly why.

Some kids are really fun and easy to be with. They always seem happy and like to do many different things. It seems like everyone wants to be their friends.

Other kids are difficult to be with. They may be grumpy, irritable, or critical. They may tease or bully other kids. You might wish you could avoid kids like these, but sometimes that is impossible.

It is a good idea to learn how to deal with difficult kids (and difficult adults, too). When you learn how to deal with difficult people, you can get along with just about everyone!

For You to Do

Think of someone you have to deal with on a regular basis and have a hard time getting along with. Without using names, make a list of things that bother you about this person.

____

____

____

Why do think this person is so difficult?

____

____

Does the way you act toward this person cause problems? Explain your answer.

____

____

____

List four new things you could do or say to try to keep the peace with this person.

1. ____

2. ____

3. ____

4. ____

... And More to Do!

Do you think most other kids would agree that this person is difficult?

____

____

____

What makes you think so?

____

____

____

How do difficult people sometimes make life harder for themselves?

____

____

____

Think of someone most kids like to be with. How does that person act?

____

____

____

Clubs and Cliques Activity 37

For You to Know

Clubs and cliques are different. They both involve kids who have an interest in common, but clubs are open to kids who share that interest, while cliques are closed to many kids, even when they want to join.

Cliques are a fact of life. You have probably found cliques at school, and grown-ups sometimes even find cliques at work. Members of a clique have something in common. For example, they may all be super popular or be on the basketball team. What makes a clique different from other social groups is the idea that it excludes kids from joining. Also, clique members often act as if they are better than those outside the group.

Clubs usually welcome new members, and there are many types of clubs that kids can join. There are computer clubs, magic clubs, fan clubs, and community service clubs. There are probably lots of clubs in your community that you could join, or you might want to start your own club!

For You to Do

In the space below, draw a picture of your clubhouse. Put the name of the club on a sign in front of the clubhouse.

Who would you invite to be in your club?

____

____

____

What will you do at your meetings?

____

____

____

... *And More to Do!*

Think of a clique at your school. What do all the kids in this group have in common with one another?

Now think of the individual kids in this clique. How are they different from one another?

When you think about the clique members as individuals, how does your view of the group change?

Would you rather be part of a club or a clique? Tell why.

Activity 38 Keeping the Peace

For You to Know

Kids don't always get along. Sometimes you may be directly involved in the disagreement, and sometimes you may be watching from the sidelines. There are ways to get involved in other kids' disagreements that can help keep the peace.

Now that you've thought a lot about how to notice and manage your own feelings, and how to understand better what other kids might be feeling in different situations, it's time to practice an even trickier skill. Helping others to resolve their problems is a really important skill, but one that can be difficult.

For You to Do

Squirrel and Bird are having a serious disagreement over a tree branch in the park. Squirrel likes to run along the branch to build up speed so that he can jump to the roof of the community center and collect the acorns that fall there. Bird has chosen the same branch to build her nest, because it is just the right height and has the perfect amount of shade.

On the lines below, write two plans for how Squirrel and Bird can settle this problem.

Plan #1

____

____

____

____

____

____

Plan #2

____

____

____

____

____

____

... And More to Do!

Describe an actual disagreement between two kids you know.

____

____

____

____

Can you think of a peacemaking strategy to help them get beyond their disagreement?

____

____

____

____

What are some of the reactions they might have if you try to help? These reactions might be good or bad.

____

____

____

____

Apologizing

Activity 39

For You to Know

We all make mistakes or forget to do things we've promised to do. Learning how and when to apologize can go a long way toward keeping your friendships smooth.

You've probably had to apologize in one way or another many times. Apologies come in all sizes, big and small. You might apologize to someone in the supermarket for bumping into them accidentally or you might apologize to a friend for breaking a promise.

"I'm sorry" is one of the most complicated things we say to one another. Depending on how they are said, those two words can sound sympathetic, sincere, sarcastic, fake, or mean. The tone of voice we use matters a lot and so does the way we hold our bodies.

For You to Do

Write a letter of apology to a friend, family member, or anyone else to whom you feel you owe an apology. It might be for something that happened recently or something that happened further in the past. It might be something you've never apologized for or something you feel you could have done a better job apologizing for.

... And More to Do!

How did you feel writing your letter of apology?

____

____

Think of a time when someone sincerely apologized to you for something that had really upset you. How did the apology make you feel?

____

____

Did it help you to forgive that person?

____

____

____

How could you tell this apology was sincere?

____

____

____

Activity 40 Compromising

For You to Know

Often we want one thing, and the people around us want something different. Compromising means meeting in the middle between what you want and what others want. In a good compromise, everyone walks away pretty happy.

Kathy and Kayla were friends, but sometimes they disagreed about what to do. One day Kayla's mom offered to take them out for lunch and asked them to decide where to go. Soon she heard them arguing. "Pizza!" Kathy insisted in a loud voice. In a louder voice, Kayla said, "No! I want a hamburger!"

Kayla's mom listened for a while, then came into the room and said, "Why don't you two come up with a compromise? Think of a way to meet in the middle."

The girls thought about it. Then Kathy said, "I know! We can go to the mall and have lunch at the food court. That way, you can have a hamburger, and I can have pizza."

"Great idea!" said Kayla. They went off to the mall and they all enjoyed their lunches.

For You to Do

Below are three columns. In the first column is a list of what Kathy would like, and in the middle column are the things Kayla would like. Can you think of a compromise for each situation?

Kathy Wants to ...	Kayla Wants to ...	The Compromise
Eat lunch at a pizza restaurant.	Eat lunch at a hamburger restaurant.	Eat lunch at a food court where they can each get what they want.
Go to the park.	Watch a movie.	
Bake cookies at their sleepover.	Play board games at their sleepover.	
Take ballet lessons with Kayla.	Take skating lessons with Kathy.	
Invite their friend Stephanie to come over.	Invite their friend Taylor to come over.	

... And More to Do!

Can you add some of your own recent compromises?

What You Wanted	What the Other Person Wanted	The Compromise

Lawrence E. Shapiro, PhD, is a nationally recognized child psychologist who is known for his innovative play-oriented techniques. He has written over two dozen books and created over forty therapeutic games. Dr. Shapiro is the founder of the Childswork/Childsplay catalog and publishing company, a leading distributor of psychologically oriented toys and games. He is the author of numerous books, including *How to Raise a Child with a High EQ: A Parents' Guide to Emotional Intelligence* and *The Secret Language of Children.*

Julia Holmes is a freelance writer living in New York City. She is the author of *100 New Yorkers: A Guide to Illustrious Lives and Locations.* Julia holds a master's degree in creative writing from Columbia University.